Shine

WRITTEN BY M. H. CLARK ✦ DESIGN & ILLUSTRATION BY JILL LABIENIEC

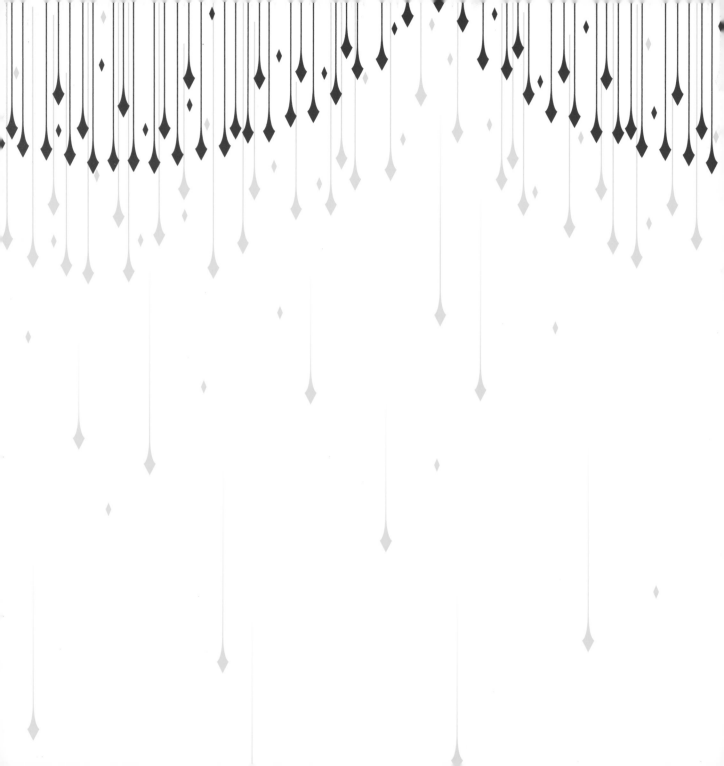

There's something about you that people notice right away.

It's a light that beams outward and brightens everything it touches. It's a glow that makes everything more vibrant.

This light is always there. And it turns on any time you're feeling confident or full of possibility. It's the light of a person who's doing good in the world, by being fully, richly, and beautifully alive.

Show this light—it's the best that is in you and your gift to give the world. Feel bold and bright in all you have to offer. And always remember to shine.

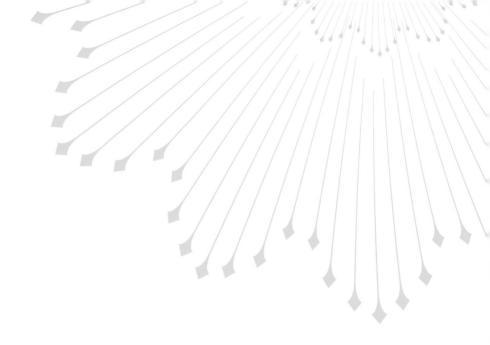

...she just had a presence, an energy,

A SORT OF LIGHT

coming from within her...

–KEVYN AUCOIN

IT'S A FAR *brighter* WORLD BECAUSE YOU'RE IN IT.

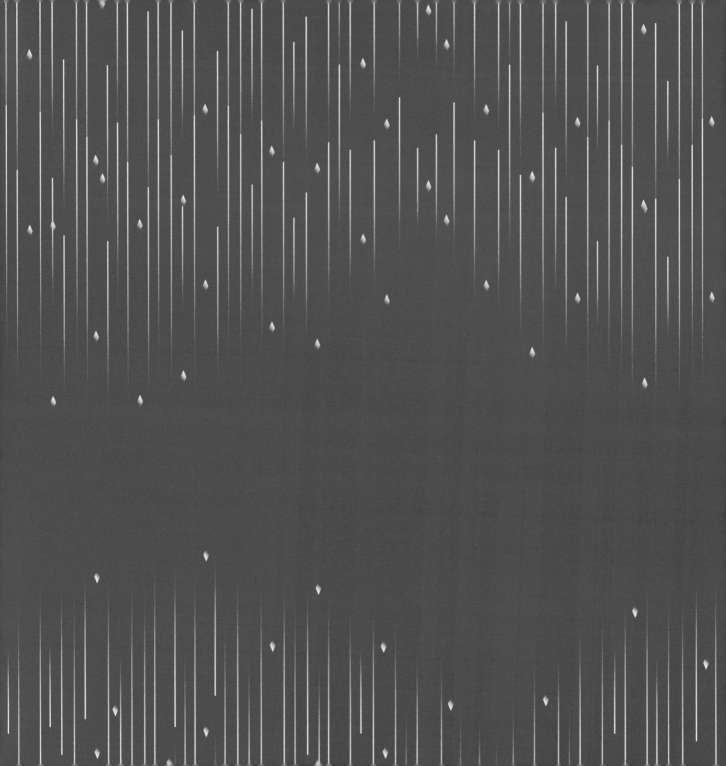

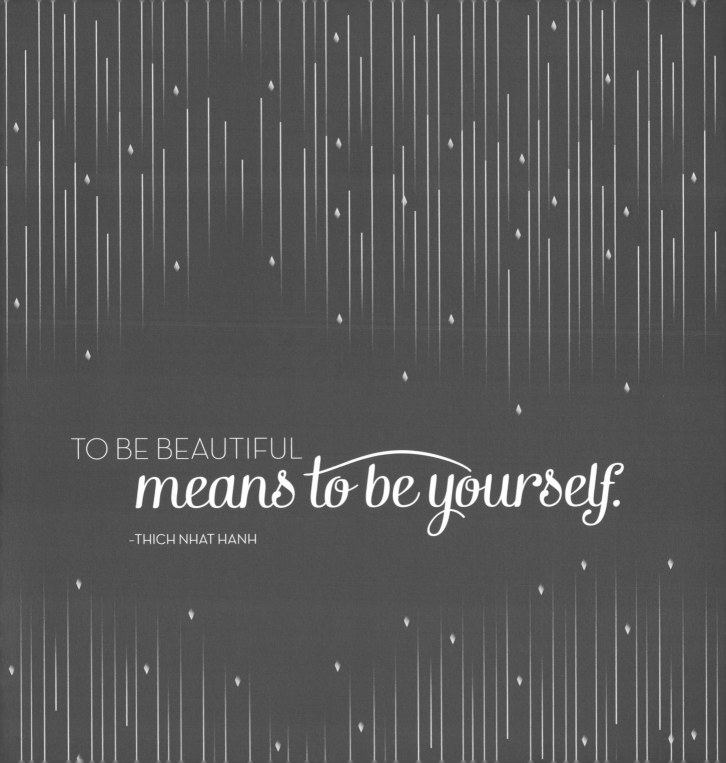

TO BE BEAUTIFUL
means to be yourself.

-THICH NHAT HANH

Radiance is the way you were made. It is the very fabric *of your being.*

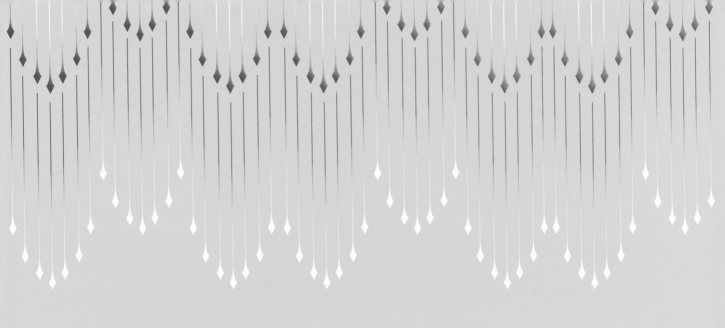

...find that phosphorescence,
THAT LIGHT WITHIN...

–EMILY DICKINSON

When you cannot
be a sun,
be a star.

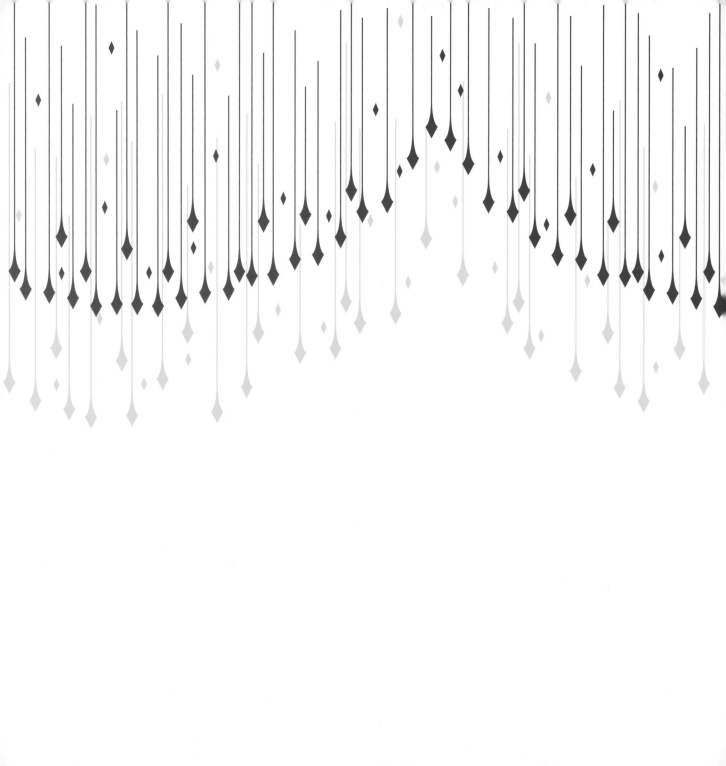

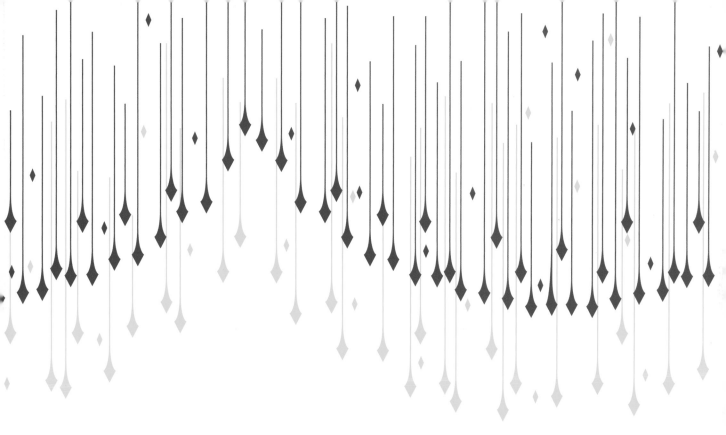

IT IS OUR PRIVILEGE &
OUR ADVENTURE TO
DISCOVER OUR OWN
SPECIAL LIGHT.

-Evelyn Dunbar

Light is not rare
WHEN YOU KNOW
WHERE TO FIND IT.

There is a candle in **your heart,** ready to be kindled.

–RUMI

NEVER PASS UP A
chance to glow.

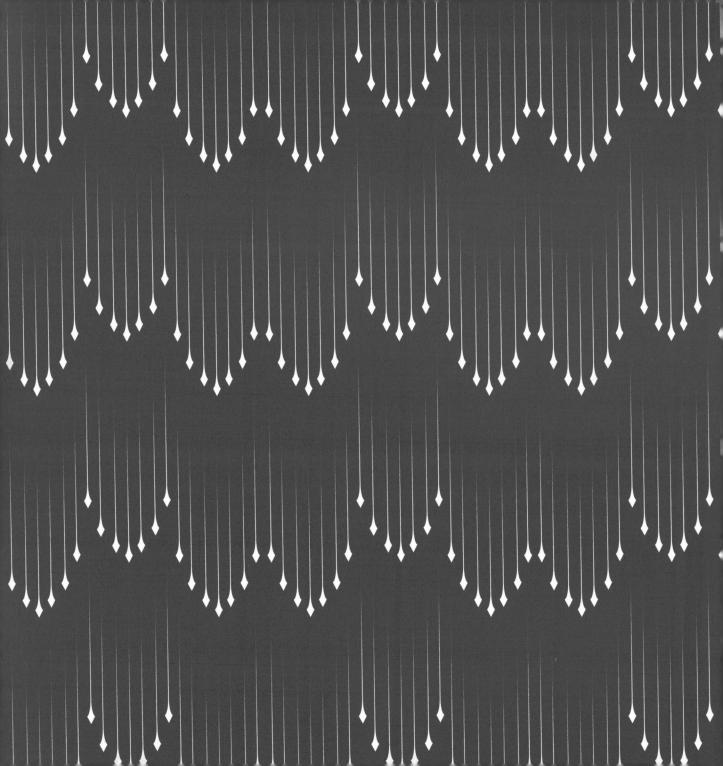

Shine

WITH ALL YOU HAVE.

–KATELYN S. IRONS

The brighter your light,
THE FURTHER IT TRAVELS.

Dream big, dare greatly, and shine brightly.

–ROBIN SIEGER

LIVE TO LET YOUR
brilliance show.

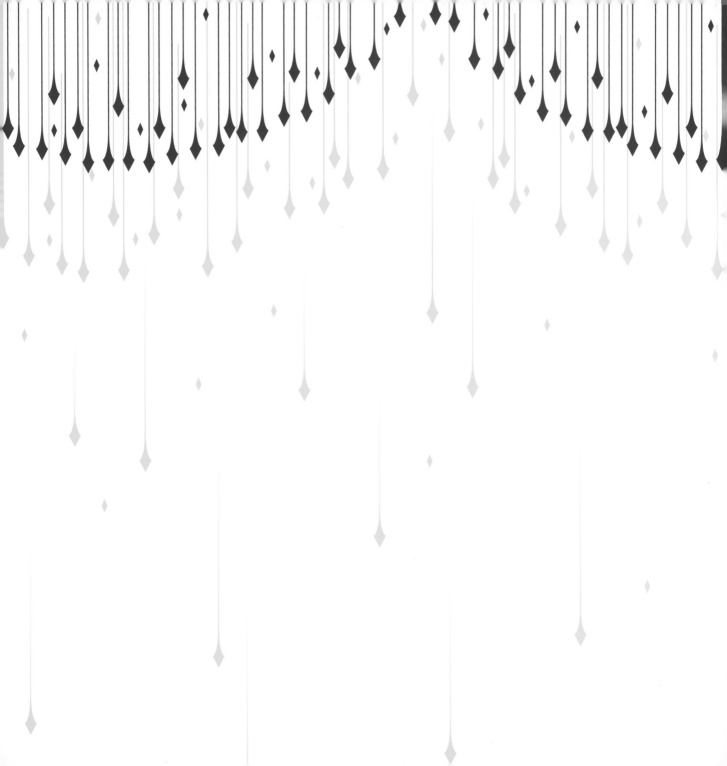

...THE PURPOSE OF LIGHT IS
TO CREATE MORE LIGHT...

-Paulo Coelho

Paint yourself
A BRIGHTER WORLD.

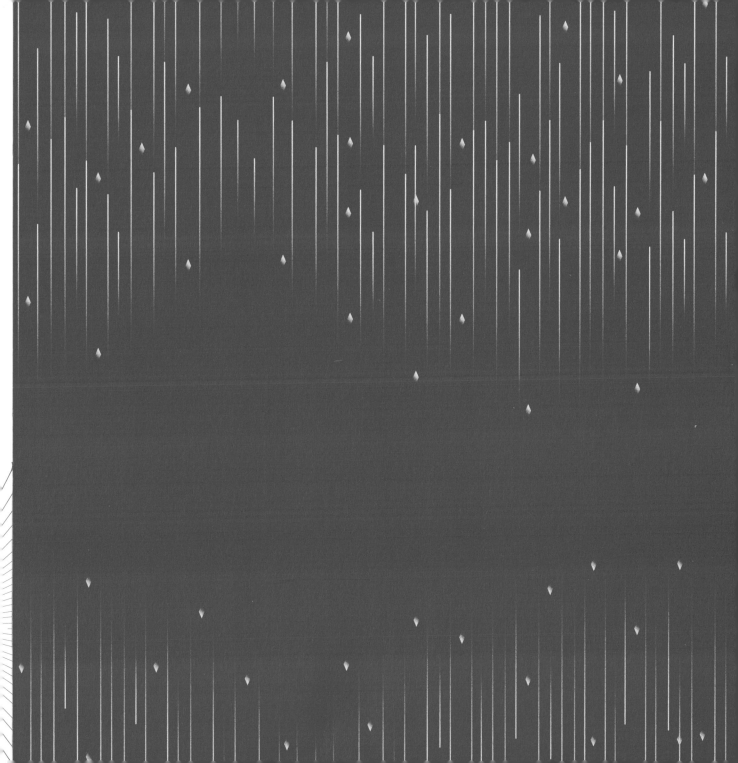

Sometimes,
MORE SPARKLE
is just the right thing.

I WANT A BRIGHTER WORD THAN

bright...

–JOHN KEATS

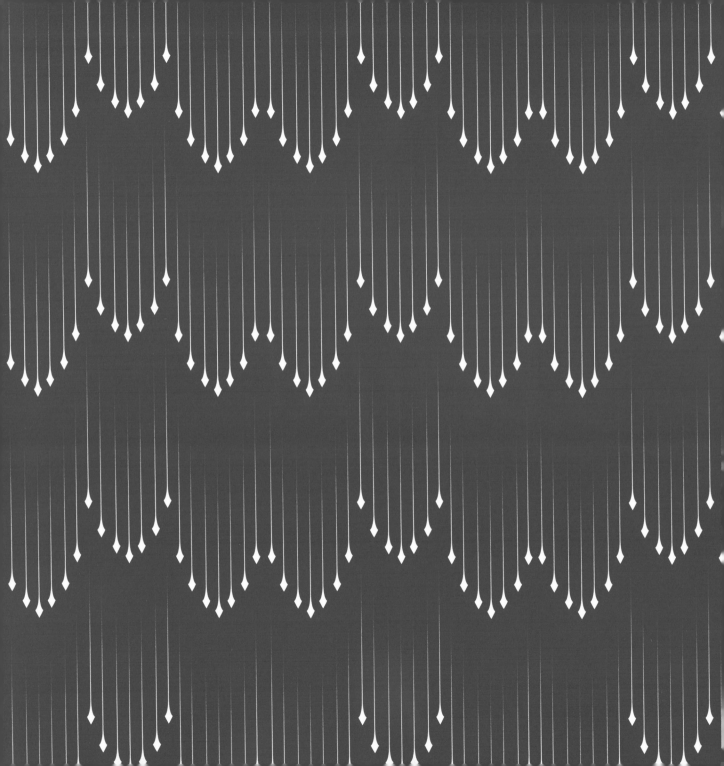

YOUR SHINE IS NOT
SIMPLY SEEN, IT IS FELT.

LIGHT TOMORROW
with today.

-ELIZABETH BARRETT BROWNING

Just by living, you brighten the way.

KEEP SHINING,

my bright and shining star of a friend.

-IVY BAKER PRIEST

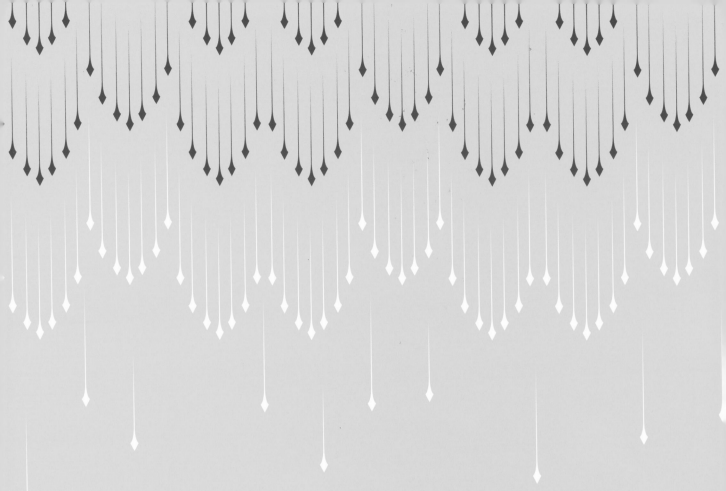

You are not simply bright around your edges,

YOU ARE BRIGHT STRAIGHT THROUGH.

...I at last discovered that there was

WITHIN ME

an invincible summer.

–ALBERT CAMUS

Always keep your fire lit.

ALWAYS KEEP YOUR HEART AGLOW.

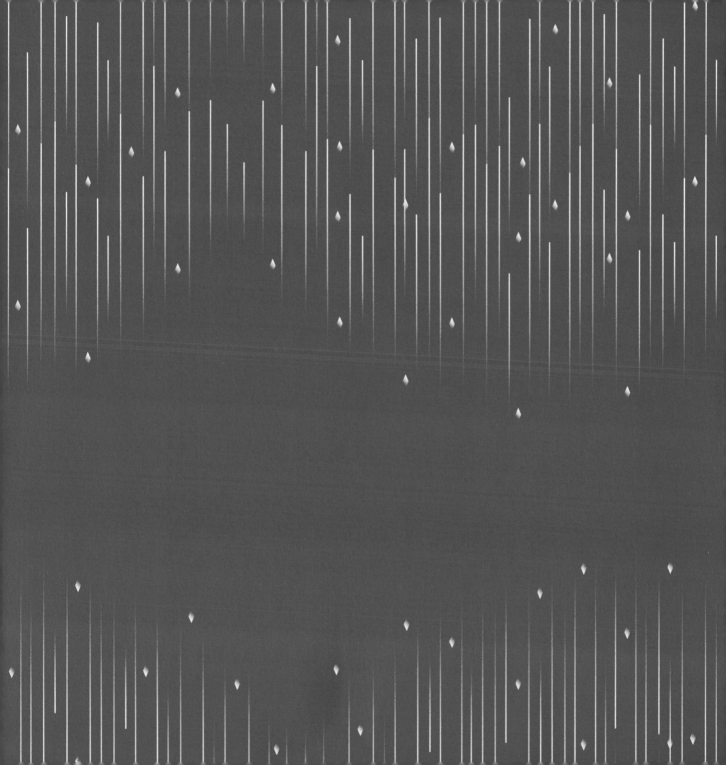

Everything is made of light...

-DON MIGUEL RUIZ

Be brilliant.
The world needs you.

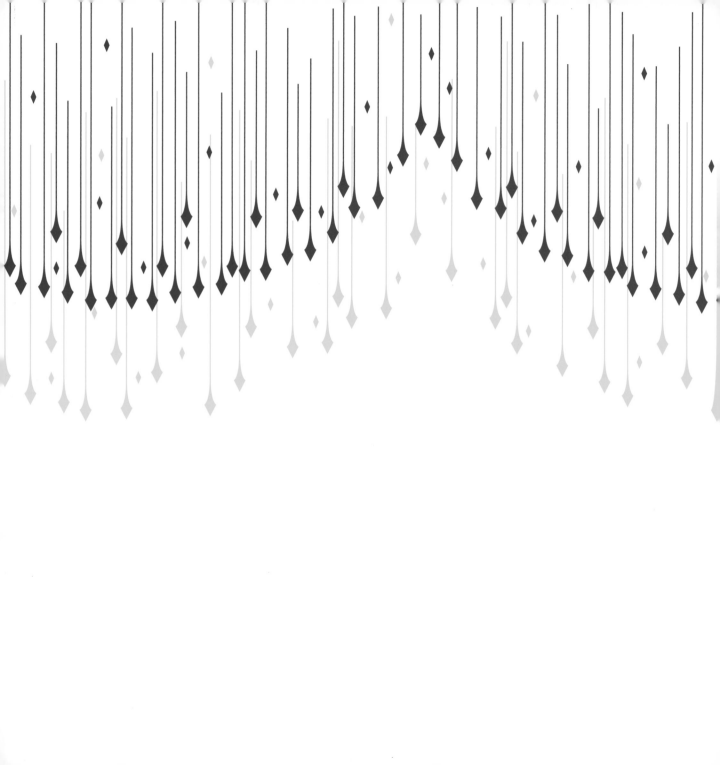

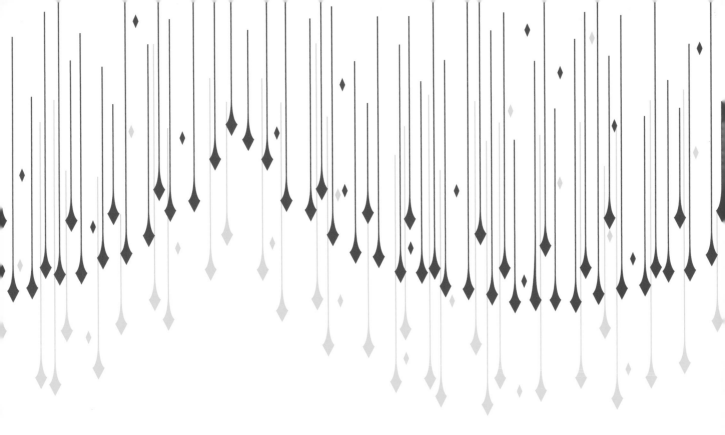

YOU ARE A CHILD OF THE UNIVERSE,
NO LESS THAN THE TREES AND THE STARS.

– Max Ehrmann

Your shine touches hearts and minds.
IT CHANGES THE WORLD.

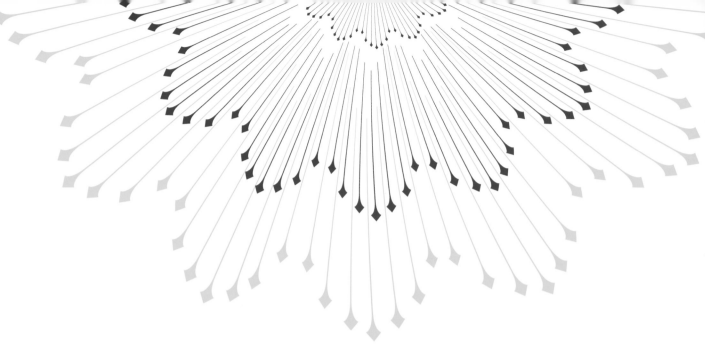

COMPENDIUM®
live inspired.

With special thanks to the entire Compendium family.

Credits:

Written by: M.H. Clark
Design & Illustration by: Jill Labieniec
Edited by: Amelia Riedler
Creative Direction by: Julie Flahiff

ISBN 978-1-938298-25-7

1st printing. Printed in China with soy and metallic inks.